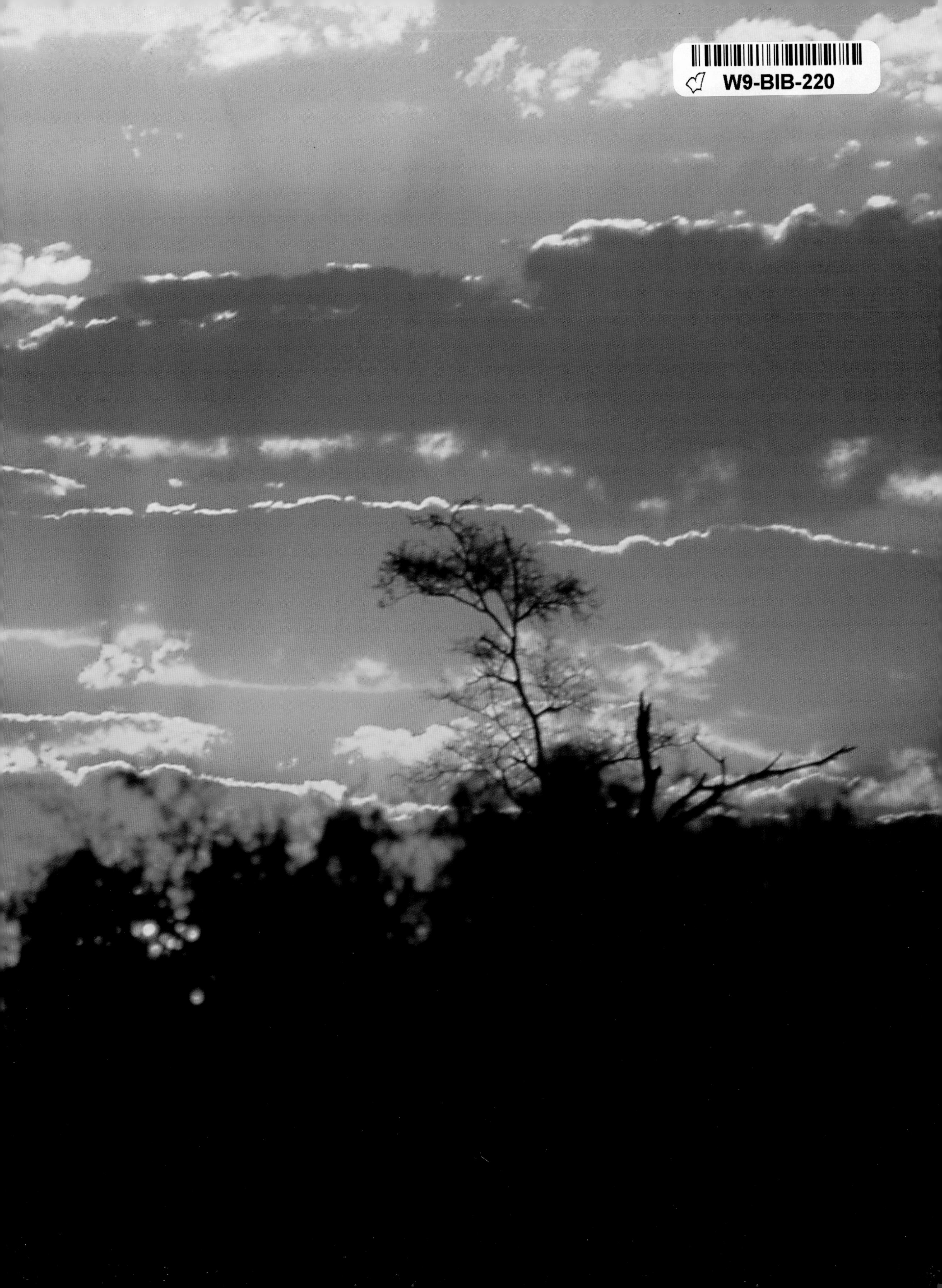

JOURNEY
into
AFRICA
A Nature Discovery Trip

Tim Knight

OXFORD
UNIVERSITY PRESS

For Mum and Dad - T.C.K.

OXFORD
UNIVERSITY PRESS

Oxford New York

Athens Auckland Bangkok Bogotá Buenos Aires Cape Town
Chennai Dar es Salaam Delhi Florence Hong Kong Istanbul
Karachi Kolkata Kuala Lumpur Madrid Melbourne Mexico City
Mumbai Nairobi Paris São Paulo Shanghai Singapore Taipei
Tokyo Toronto Warsaw

with associated companies in Berlin Ibadan
Published by Oxford University Press, Inc.
198 Madison Avenue, New York, New York 10016
www.oup-usa.org

Oxford is a registered trade mark of Oxford University Press

Library of Congress Cataloging-in-Publication Data is available.

ISBN 0-19-521845-0

1 3 5 7 9 10 8 6 4 2

Printed in Hong Kong

With grateful thanks to the
following organizations:

NOMAD African Travel
Smugglers Cottage, Church Road, Westbourne,
Emsworth, Hampshire PO10 8UA, UK
www.nomadafricantravel.co.uk

Oasis Safaris, Botswana
www.oasis-safari.com

Okavango Tours & Safaris
www.okavango.com

Contents

Safe Journey!

Picture a land of vast deserts, deep lakes, thick forests, winding rivers, muddy swamps, and snow-capped mountains. Imagine a place where huge elephants, lightning-quick cheetahs, and sky-scraping giraffes are free to roam across the open plains. This is Africa, home to the biggest, fastest, and tallest four-legged creatures on earth. An African safari is like a journey through a fantasy world. It offers the chance to meet amazing animals that we can usually see only in a zoo or on our television screens.

▶ We will need to travel by canoe for part of the journey.

Going on safari is a serious business. We can make it safer and more enjoyable by being well prepared. Choosing the right clothes and equipment is very important. We need shots, too, to protect us from Africa's many dangerous diseases. Insect repellent and some nasty-tasting tablets will help us to avoid catching malaria, a dangerous fever carried by mosquitoes. Swimming may not be safe. The tiny water snails found in some lakes are more dangerous than a crocodile. They carry bilharzia, a microscopic worm that can cause serious illness if it finds its way inside the human body.

A wide-brimmed hat gives all-around protection against the burning sun

Binoculars help us to see animals that are far away

Dark colors blend in with the natural landscape

Long pants and sleeves help to avoid scratches and bites

Walking boots with thick soles protect the feet from sharp rocks, thorns, and snakes

It's difficult to spot wildlife while playing computer games

Baseball caps cannot give full protection from the sun

◀ A four-wheel drive vehicle is essential for the rough terrain.

Searching for wild animals is very exciting, but we must know what to do when we meet them, especially if we are on foot. Lion cubs may look cuddly, but their parents are fierce killers. A mother elephant will even charge a truck to protect her baby. We have to be ready for anything and remember to do exactly as the guide tells us.

White is a warning color that scares the animals

As long as we follow the rules, this will be a great adventure. Now that we know what to take and how to behave, let's find out more about the journey.

Leave behind the loud music and listen to the noises of Africa instead

Bare arms and legs will be cut badly

Designer sneakers are no use on a rough safari

▲ We will need tents, mosquito nets, sleeping bags, and flashlights at night; backpacks, sun-screen, and water bottles during the day.

Safari
Guide

Victoria falls

airstrip

village

Safari is a Swahili word. It means "long and difficult journey." In the past, this often meant a dangerous hunting trip. These days, most people go on safari to watch animals, not to shoot them. But watching animals is only part of the adventure. First, we have to find them.

Our journey will take us over steaming waterfalls, into crocodile-infested lakes, past sandy deserts, and across dusty plains stretching as far as the eye can see. Traveling in Africa is hard work. In the dry season, the roads are bumpy and thick with dust. When the rains finally arrive, the tracks turn to deep, sticky mud. It is not possible to drive quickly. The best way to see animals is to camp somewhere deep in the bush, far away from busy towns, noisy people, and mobile phones. When we finally reach the campsite many hours later, there will be no hot showers, flushing toilets, or junk food.

Does it sound like fun to bounce around in a truck for days on end, feeling hot, tired, bruised and dirty? How about canoeing past a bad-tempered hippo? Or sneaking up on a thirsty elephant? Still interested? Let's go on safari!

river

hippo encounter

first camp

dry riverbed

game drive

lion encounter

bush fire

second camp

water hole

The Smoke that
Thunders

In the distance, a long line of white smoke seems to be rising, like a huge fire stretching across the horizon. In fact, the "smoke" is spray from one of the world's largest waterfalls. We are about to fly over Victoria Falls. The powerful Zambezi River flows through the heart of Africa. In places where hard rock and soft rock meet, the river cuts deeper into the softer rock, slowly wearing it away. At Victoria Falls, the river has carved out a spectacular cliff, 325 feet high and nearly 1.25 miles wide.

▶ The magnificent view through the window of a small plane makes up for the bumpy flight.

◀ Vultures have amazing eyesight. They can spot a dead animal from high above the ground.

Leaving behind the smoking waterfall, the plane passes over a huge bird. The tips of its long wings look like outstretched fingers. Gliding high above the ground, vultures make flying look easy. But getting off the ground in the first place is not quite so simple for these heavy birds. They must wait until the day warms up, so they can hitch a ride on the hot air currents that rise from the ground. Once airborne, they can spend hours soaring high in the sky, on the lookout for an easy meal.

Far below, a big, gray animal is wading into a river. Is that an elephant? Too late. The view through the window changes suddenly from muddy brown to bright blue, as the plane dips sideways. With one wing pointing skyward and the other toward the ground, we start our descent. The pilot is landing. Fasten your seat belts!

◀ In times of flood, 16 million cubic feet of water plunge over Victoria Falls every minute.

◀ The local name for Victoria Falls is *mosi-oa-tunya*, meaning "smoke that thunders."

9

High Noon

The plane touches down, bounces along the airstrip, and comes to a halt in a cloud of dust. A jeep is waiting nearby, ready for the long drive to our first camp. After unpacking, it is tempting to start exploring straight away, but this is no time for a long walk. The sun burns brightly overhead. Even through thick boots, the ground feels baking hot. There is plenty of shade under the big acacia trees. Beyond them lies a vast lake, whose surface dazzles in the bright sunlight.

10

The camp is filled with the buzzing, whining, and trumpeting of insects. The most ear-splitting sound comes from the cicadas. These insects call to each other by making a very fast rattling sound, using a part of their body called a tymbal. Apart from the insect noise, there is not much sign of life. In the heat of the day, most warm-blooded animals try to keep cool by resting in the shade.

There is a loud rustling noise close by. A monitor lizard, over a yard long, scuttles out of sight behind a tree trunk. Like all reptiles, lizards spend hours sunbathing.

▲ Eye spy! Jumping spiders have excellent eyesight to help them hunt.

◄ A colorful dragonfly rests on a lakeside twig, waiting to ambush a passing insect.

Until their bodies have warmed up, they are too slow to catch food or escape their enemies. Every morning, they bask on their favorite rock, but even reptiles have to find shelter from the scorching midday sun. Most animals are active early in the morning and again in the late afternoon, when the day is cooler. Until then, the best thing to do is to find a quiet corner and join in the siesta.

▶ Monitor lizards will eat almost anything, from birds' eggs and small animals to rotting meat. They even swim or climb trees to find food.

Walking on *Water*

By late afternoon, the sun is lower in the sky. This is a perfect time to take a short boat trip and explore the edge of the lake. Animals come down to the water's edge to feed on the juicy grasses. We sit quietly in the canoe, hoping to sneak up on them. A loud snort tells the guide that a buffalo is feeding nearby. He paddles away quickly. It is wise to keep a safe distance from a bad-tempered buffalo.

▶ A jacana walks across the lake's surface, using the floating leaves for support.

▼ Crocodiles have lived on Earth since the time of the dinosaurs.

Beyond the reed bed, a crocodile is lying on the muddy bank. Its huge mouth is wide open. A small bird lands on the crocodile's nose, then hops inside its mouth and begins pecking among the teeth, picking out bits of food. The crocodile allows its visitor to continue feeding. It has learned that a walking toothbrush is more useful than a bird-sized snack.

▲ A green carpet of waterlilies bursts into flower on the water's surface.

▶ Who's been sleeping in my reedbed? A cattle egret settles down for the night.

We drift on through a patch of waterlily leaves, called lily pads. A jacana bird is using them as stepping stones. Jacanas are also known as lily-trotters, because their long toes and enormous feet help them to walk on the floating plants. As the sun goes down, the guide paddles back towards the camp. Birds are starting to gather in flocks among the reeds for the night. This keeps them safe from nighttime hunters.

Call of the
Wild

An African sunset is an unforgettable sight. Some evenings the whole sky glows bright orange, as though it is on fire.

▶ Camping in Africa is a great adventure, but some people prefer to sleep in a comfortable lodge.

At dusk, when the sun has just disappeared below the horizon, biting insects such as mosquitoes start to appear. Some female *Anopheles* mosquitoes carry malaria, a dangerous tropical disease. In the evening, it is best to use insect repellent and wear pants and long-sleeved shirts to avoid being bitten. Back at camp, we eat a tasty supper of chicken and rice, cooked on an open fire. Everyone is tired.

▲ A flock of open-billed storks roosts in the safety of a dead tree.

Before long we are all safely tucked up in our sleeping bags, under a mosquito net. After zipping up the tent flaps to keep out scorpions and snakes, we lie back and gaze out through the tent window. There are no lights in the middle of the African bush, so the stars are much brighter there. It looks as though a giant diamond has exploded into a million pieces, showering the night sky with brilliant jewels.

Somewhere in the darkness, an owl hoots. There is a rustling outside the tent. The creatures of the night are stirring. We fall asleep with the bleeping and croaking of a thousand frogs ringing in our ears. Later, a rumbling noise wakes the whole camp. At first, it sounds like distant thunder. As it draws closer, it turns into a loud roar, so close to the tent that the ground seems to shake. Silence. Even the frogs seem to be listening. But the roaring has stopped. The visitor has already left.

▲ Unlike most owls, the pearl-spotted owl is often seen during daylight.

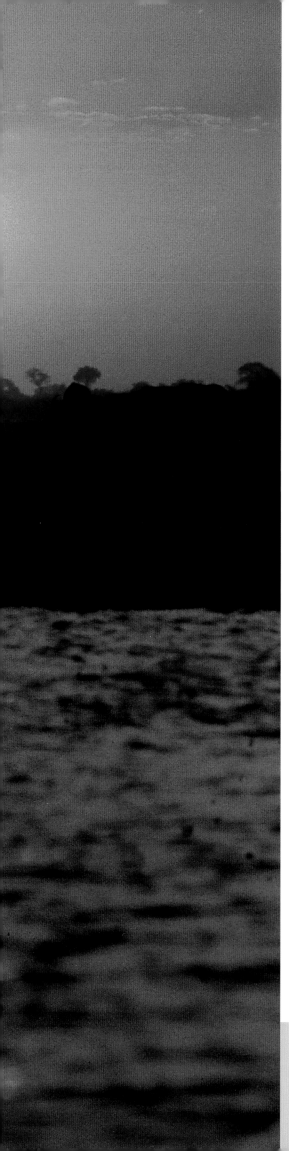

◄ The sun sets behind a herd of grazing buffalo.

► A painted reed frog, smaller than a person's thumbnail, flattens itself against a plant stem.

The Early
Bird

Before the first light of dawn, the noises of the night have already faded away. Now the air is filled instead with squawking, whistling, and shrieking, as birds and monkeys start to wake up. Africa is no place for those who like to sleep in. There is a feeling of excitement in the camp. Someone heard lions roaring during the night. So that's what it was! The jeep's engine is already running. We're off to look for lions.

Our guide, Cisco, drives slowly, stopping regularly to check the ground for animal footprints. Could one of those sandy rocks in the distance be a sleeping lion? It is a dusty ride, because there has been no rain for many months. Most of the rivers have disappeared, too. We reach a steep bank. During last year's rains there was a raging torrent here, too deep for a vehicle to cross. Now there is only a dry riverbed.

▲ Although a giraffe's neck is incredibly long, it has just seven bones connecting its head to its body, the same number as humans.

Among the nearby acacia trees, a few branches are shaking. A long-necked, spindly-legged creature is tugging at a mouthful of leaves high in the treetops. Adult giraffes are taller than a telephone pole and can reach the highest branches. A giraffe needs a very big heart to pump blood all the way to its head. Its tongue is as rough as sandpaper, so it has no problem chewing the sharp acacia thorns.

▶ An acacia tree grows sharp thorns to protect its leaves.

▲ A giraffe's tongue is over 16 inches long.

▲ A baby zebra can recognize its mother by the pattern of her stripes.

A bird with beautiful, rainbow-colored feathers calls loudly from its perch in a dead tree. A second bird flies overhead, diving and rolling in midair. Like fighter pilots showing off, these lilac-breasted rollers are displaying to each other above their territory, the place where they have made a home.

A herd of relaxed-looking zebras watches the vehicle for a few moments, before continuing to graze on the dry grass. They would be more nervous if the lions were close by. Zebras may all look the same to us, but each one has a different stripe pattern, as unique as a human fingerprint. When it feeds among bushes or long grass, a zebra is surprisingly hard to see, because its stripes help to disguise the shape of its body.

▲ The lilac-breasted roller is the national bird of Botswana.

▲ Walking with heads upside down, flamingos use their beaks like sieves to collect their microscopic food.

Let's Stick
Together

Zebras are not the only animals that live in large groups. Birds come together for food as well as safety. Millions of flamingos gather on lakes and salt pans to feed on tiny algae, the miniature plants that grow in the water. Seen from a distance, a flamingo flock looks like a giant pink stain spreading through the water, as though someone has spilled the world's biggest pail of paint.

► Early warning system. A female impala keeps watch while others feed.

A herd of impalas, a common type of antelope, is grazing quietly nearby. They don't all feed at once. Some of them look around nervously and snort loudly at the slightest sign of danger. With so many ears, eyes, and noses on red alert, the herd is unlikely to be taken by surprise. Even if a lion or cheetah attacks, each impala has a better chance of escaping as part of a big group.

Animals that hunt, called predators, sometimes stick together too. Wild dogs hunt in packs. When they chase an antelope herd, they look closely for a weak or injured animal. Once they spot one, they take turns snapping at its heels and biting it until it is too tired to run any farther. With their needle-sharp teeth, a pack of wild dogs can eat a whole antelope in five minutes.

We spot a thorn tree nearby that is full of birds' nests. These belong to weavers, sparrow-like birds that often live in large, noisy colonies. They build their nests by weaving and knotting together pieces of grass. An expert can tell what kind of weaver lives in a colony just by looking at the shape of the nests.

◄ Safety in numbers. A colony of buffalo weavers in an overcrowded tree.

► A wild dog is ready for the hunt after a long rest.

Family
Fortunes

It's lunchtime. Cisco stops the truck under a shady tree. As we are eating, a yellow-billed hornbill lands nearby, looking exactly like Zasu in *The Lion King*. He picks up a scrap of bread and carries it to a tree hole, where his mate is sitting on a nest. The entrance is almost completely blocked with hard mud, but he can still feed her through a narrow gap. She will not leave the hole until her eggs have hatched.

A group of baboons, Africa's largest monkey, is feeding under the trees. Baboons live together in big families, known as troops, containing up to a hundred monkeys. A huge male baboon has climbed a tree. He sits and watches from his lookout position. He may look like the boss, but the females are really in charge. When the baboons move from place to place, the oldest females travel in the middle, protected by the rest of the troop. The youngest babies hitch a ride on one of the grown-ups, riding like jockeys or hanging underneath.

▼ The yellow-billed hornbill has learned to hang around campsites looking for scraps of food.

▲ Monkey business. Young baboons play "king of the castle" in a fallen tree.

▼ Young giraffes grow very quickly, doubling their height in only one year.

Even the fiercest creatures can be gentle parents. After laying her eggs, a crocodile guards them until they have hatched, then picks up all her tiny babies in her mouth and carries them down to the safety of the water. When a baby elephant is born, the whole herd gathers around to watch. As the calf grows, all the older elephants help the mother to look after it.

Some youngsters are not so lucky. As we are driving back toward camp, we pass a baby antelope, standing alone and shivering with fright. A predator will soon kill him unless his mother finds him first.

◀ Some baby elephants hardly leave their mother's side until they are nearly 10 years old.

Campfire
Stories

Back in camp, as darkness falls, a hamerkop flies back to its treetop nest. Many tribes believe it is a bird of ill omen, bringing bad luck to those who see it. Some will even burn down their house if a hamerkop flies over it. Most stories are spoken out loud, not written down. Cisco tells us the hippopotamus story that he first heard from his grandfather:

At first the other animals did not want the hippo to live in the river, because they thought he would eat all the fish. To prove to them that he only ate grass, the hippo promised to spray his dung on to the bushes whenever he came out of the water, so that they could check it for signs of fish bones!

▼ A hippo can eat up to 130 pounds of grass in a single night.

◀ The smells of the campfire may attract hyenas and other uninvited guests.

▲ The puff adder is responsible for three-quarters of all snakebite injuries in Africa.

"Hippopotamus" is a strange word, but it just means "river horse." Animal and plant names come from different languages. When Dutch farmers settled in Africa, they named the hamerkop after the shape of its head. In their language, Afrikaans, hamerkop means "hammer head." Once we have seen a shoebill, a sausage tree, or a bat-eared fox, funny names make more sense.

During supper, Cisco tells stories about Africa's dangerous snakes. He talks about the deadly spitting cobra, which spits poison to defend itself, aiming at the eyes. We shiver as he describes the giant, 20-foot-long pythons that can squeeze a large antelope to death and swallow it whole. Finally, we hear that the highly poisonous puff adder likes to crawl inside warm sleeping bags. This could be a sleepless night!

Hippo Attack

After breakfast, Cisco tells us that we will be spending the day on the river. As we climb into the canoe, a troop of baboons sneaks into the camp, hoping to steal some food. They have learned how to unzip bags and tent flaps.

Slowly Cisco paddles us up the river. The water is full of crocodiles, but these are not the only danger. The hippopotamus kills more people than any other animal in Africa. Although they eat plants, not meat, they will attack anything that comes too close. Hippos only leave the river in the cool evening. During the day, they stay in the water to protect their bare skin from the burning sun, with just their ears, eyes and nostrils poking above the surface. Sometimes they disappear completely, holding their breath for up to five minutes. Hippos are like icebergs: The most dangerous part is often out of sight.

◀ A male baboon bares his long canine teeth to frighten his rivals.

◀ Before eating a bee or wasp, a bee-eater rubs it against a branch to remove the stinger.

Multicolored birds twist and turn in mid air. These are bee-eaters. They catch insects in their long, curved beaks, and carry the food back to their nests in the sandy riverbank. Most bee-eaters are gregarious, which means that they live together in flocks.

A fish eagle swoops down and plucks a fish out of the water with its feet. Bubbles are rising next to the canoe. Suddenly, a gigantic head pops up right beside us, followed by 6,600 pounds of full-grown hippopotamus. Like an erupting volcano, the hippo opens its massive jaws, yawns loudly, and lifts itself high into the air. It crashes back into the water and almost capsizes the canoe as Cisco paddles away. That was just a warning. A really angry hippo would have bitten our canoe in half!

▲ A yawning hippo warns us to keep our distance.

▲ A fish eagle's feet are tipped with needle-sharp talons that help it to grab hold of a slippery fish.

You Scratch
My Back...

As we leave behind the disgruntled hippo, we pass a hamerkop at the water's edge. This bird often shares its home with a deadly snake. The cool, dark inside of a hamerkop nest is the perfect place for a black mamba to sleep. Mambas mainly eat rats, so the bird is in no danger, and its roommate will frighten away any nest robbers. The snake is not just a guest. It is a bodyguard and babysitter, too.

Nearby, a male warthog is rolling in the mud. Wallowing like this helps him to keep cool, and the coat of mud protects his skin from biting insects and blood-sucking ticks.

A tick feeds by cutting a hole in the skin, sticking in its tiny snout, and drinking the blood like lemonade through a straw. Creatures that feed on other animals are called parasites. Their victims are known as hosts. Mud wallows and dust baths are not the only way to remove parasites. Monkeys comb through each others' fur, using their fingers to pick off anything nasty. This is known as mutual grooming.

▼ The hamerkop builds one of the largest nests in the bird kingdom.

▼ The aggressive black mamba is the most feared snake in Africa.

26

▲ Cattle egrets often follow a grazing buffalo and feed on the insects disturbed by its hooves.

▶ Yellow-billed ox peckers enjoy a movable feast.

Others use a different kind of pest control. Oxpeckers, distant cousins of the starling, have learned to hitch a ride on animals and climb all over them in search of a meal. Through binoculars, we can see them clinging to a zebra's back, using their stiff tails to balance as they peck out the fat ticks. The oxpeckers use the zebra as a walking restaurant. In return, the zebra gets a free health check from its very own team of flying doctors.

Staying Alive

On the bank two male antelopes are fighting. They lock horns to test each other's strength. Before the real fighting begins, the two rivals try to work out which one is stronger just by looking and listening. Instead of biting and kicking, male giraffes neck-wrestle to decide the winner. A tired or injured animal is more likely to starve or be killed. Hunting for food or avoiding a predator takes lots of energy.

▼ The one that didn't get away. Another loser in Africa's life and death struggle.

▶ Klipspringers live among steep rocks, where most predators cannot reach them.

Predators hunt in different ways. A cheetah, the fastest animal on four legs, uses its speed; lions and leopards rely on stealth, creeping up on their prey until they are close enough to pounce. Others play a waiting game: some spiders build a web and sit tight; herons stand completely still for hours, waiting to spear a passing fish with their dagger-like beaks; the puff adder, like all vipers, lies in ambush until a rat is within striking distance.

The waiting game: a spider sits patiently until an insect flies into its web.

To escape, many animals simply run for their lives. Others climb a tree, find a burrow, or swim to safety. Some may fight back: the sable antelope can kill a lion with one backward stab from its magnificent horns; a zebra can force a crocodile to let go with a quick bite to the eye. Insects often use camouflage, disguising themselves as a leaf or twig. Most animals run, fight, or hide, but not always. Antelopes sometimes just leap into the air and bounce on all four legs. This "stotting" says to predators: "Look how strong I am. Don't bother trying to catch me."

With the current behind us, the return journey is easier. We paddle quickly past the hippos to avoid another close encounter. Back at camp we find lion footprints. Fresh ones. They must be close. There is still time for a quick drive before sunset. Let's go!

► The tsessebe, Africa's fastest antelope, can reach speeds of up to 55 mph.

29

King of the
Beasts

Around the very first bend, Cisco suddenly stops the truck. Lying in the shade, panting to cool down, is a huge lion. His magnificent golden mane is already turning black in places. Although he looks tired, he is in his prime, as fit and as strong as he will ever be.

◄ A lioness relaxes with her daughters.

A growling noise behind the truck makes us turn around. A whole group of lions, called a pride, is walking out of the bushes. There are five adult females, called lionesses, two young males, and half a dozen cubs of different ages. A lioness leads the way. She is the matriarch, the most important female, who keeps the pride in order. She yawns widely, showing the strong, sharp teeth that are so important for killing and eating. Once a lion loses its teeth, or has its jaw broken by a kick from a zebra, it will die of starvation.

A noisy flock of vultures begins fighting over the half-eaten buffalo carcass abandoned by the lions. Vultures and other scavengers like marabou storks, jackals, and hyenas are quick to arrive when lions make a kill. The big male lions always eat first. Everyone else must wait their turn. This is called a pecking order. The brave or impatient ones try to sneak in and steal a quick mouthful. A large clan of hungry hyenas may even drive off the lions before they have finished eating. Their jaws are strong enough to break up the skin and bones of any animal, even an elephant. Hyenas are like trashcans on legs. They eat almost anything, dead or alive.

▲ The marabou stork's beak is strong enough to puncture the hide of a dead buffalo.

▼ Vultures with no table manners squabble over the remains of a lion kill.

◄ Lion cubs are often left alone while the pride is hunting.

Stranded!

The lions are starting to move away. They walk slowly along the trail, their fur glowing orange in the evening sun. Cisco starts the truck and tries to follow the pride, but the wheels have sunk deep in the sand.

▶ A male impala grows nervous as darkness approaches.

He points at a bush with small pink flowers, growing next to the track. The Kalahari apple leaf can only live in loose, sandy soil. For some vehicles, this bush is nature's way of saying "no entry." Driving in deep sand takes lots of practice. This truck is meant for difficult conditions, but the place where we stopped to watch the lions is like a sandpit. We are stuck.

▼ A red-billed hornbill sunbathes among the blossoms of a Kalahari apple leaf bush.

The light is beginning to fade. It is only a short walk back to the camp, but it would be foolish to leave the vehicle. Who knows what dangerous animals are lurking in the bushes? Cisco has a better idea. He lets some air out of the tires, then asks us to clear the sand away from the wheels. By the time we have finished, it is already dark. Shining a flashlight, we can see animals hopping around like miniature kangaroos in the beam of light. These are spring hares. They leave their burrows at night to feed on grass and roots.

▲ That sinking feeling. The truck's tires begin to disappear as quickly as the setting sun.

▶ The vicious spikes of a thorn bush glow eerily in the pale moonlight.

A loud cackling noise shatters the silence. It sounds like mad laughter. Cisco's flashlight beam picks out three pairs of yellow eyes staring back at us. Hyenas! Let's go. He starts the engine, while we stand behind the truck, ready to push with all our strength. Slowly but surely, it inches forward out of the sand trap. As it picks up speed, we jump aboard and drive back to camp.

Mobile Homes

▲ Many African villages consist of a scattered collection of huts.

In the morning, the lions have moved on. It's time for us to do the same. Some animals have permanent homes. For others, home is wherever they can find food. These nomadic animals wander far and wide in search of fresh grass. Wherever they go, the predators must follow.

Outside the towns and villages, Africa still has many nomadic groups of people, too, who move from place to place. Some grow crops. Others keep cattle or goats, which provide meat, milk, cheese, and clothing. These nomads live in temporary huts, made from mud, stones, and grass, until it is time to search for fresh water or new grazing land for their animals. Some even carry their homes with them when they leave.

◀ Elephants searching for water have scraped this baobab tree trunk with their tusks.

We make our new camp near a tree that seems to be growing upside down. The baobab, or "upside down tree," is very important to the San. They turn its fruit into snacks and make musical instruments from the wood. Best of all, its trunk is swollen with precious water.

As we collect wood for the fire, a small bird appears and starts calling. It's a honeyguide. While Cisco is preparing lunch, he tells us how the honeyguide and the San help each other. Like partners in crime, they rob bees' hives together and then split the loot. A bird guides a hunter to the nest with its "follow me" call, and waits for him to smoke out the bees. The hunter takes most of the honey, leaving part of the honeycomb for the bird, which eats the bees' grubs and wax. The San believe that any honeyguide not given its share will lead the next hunter straight to a dangerous animal instead!

In the Kalahari Desert of southern Africa, the San (also called Bushmen) survive without keeping animals. Their ancestors have lived off the land for thousands of years. They hunt with spears, find fruit, dig up roots, or gather grass seed for food. The San have learned which plants are safe to eat and which are poisonous. They can also find water even in the hottest, driest places.

▶ Hunter-gatherers like the San are experts at catching animals for food.

A Walk on the
Wild Side

In the cool of late afternoon, we search for animals on foot. With no truck to hide us, they are much harder to approach. Hunted by humans for centuries, animals have learned that a human shape means danger. We must keep quiet. Cisco checks which way the wind is blowing. Most animals have an acute sense of smell. We don't want the wind to carry our scent toward their twitching noses.

▼ When tracking animals on foot, it is best to use the scattered trees and bushes as cover.

▲ These baboon tracks look just like human handprints.

A termite colony begins with just a pair of king and queen termites. After burrowing underground, the queen lays thousands of eggs, which hatch into workers and soldiers. Guarded by the soldier termites, the workers build a mud palace out of chewed earth and their own saliva. This mixture sets as hard as concrete. As well as the tall towers visible above ground, termite mounds have deep underground chambers.

Cisco has stopped again. We are standing next to an enormous pile of steaming dung. Elephants!

◀ Hyena dung is usually white because of all the calcium in the bones they eat.

◀ This termite mound is taller than a giraffe and may contain more than a million insects.

Every footprint or feather tells its own story. These hidden messages seem like a foreign language to us, but Cisco understands. He has cracked the secret code. Cisco points to some paw prints with claw marks, made by a cheetah. Most cats have retractable claws, which can be tucked away inside their paws until they are needed for fighting or catching prey. Cheetahs cannot pull in their claws, so their tracks are easy to recognize.

We pass a tall chimney of dried earth. It's a termite mound. Termites look like white ants. Their pale bodies would be fried to a crisp by the hot sun, so they only come out at night. Even then, they protect themselves from predators by building a kind of mud roof over the paths that they use. Sheltered beneath a crust of mud, they feed on dead plant material.

Jumbo Jet

Through the bushes, we can see a big bull elephant wading into a water hole. During the dry season, these pools are like powerful magnets. They attract thirsty animals from all directions. We move closer, treading carefully. Elephants have poor eyesight, but they can spot sudden movement. Even the crack of a dry twig could give us away.

Using his trunk like a vacuum, the elephant sucks up water, three gallons at a time, and squirts it down his throat. It sounds like a hose filling an empty tank. An elephant's trunk can pick berries from a bush, or rip a whole tree out of the ground. It is a living tool kit: drinking straw, power shower, telescopic arm, snorkel, fly swatter, and lethal weapon all rolled into one.

▲ The "klink, klink" call of the blacksmith plover sounds like a hammer on an anvil.

The wind changes direction. He raises his trunk to sniff the air, shakes his head, and trumpets loudly. With ears flapping, he charges toward us. Cisco doesn't move. The elephant is bluffing. If this were a real charge, he would pin back his ears and tuck in his trunk. Instead, he veers off into the bushes. With hearts still pounding, we stare at the large muddy craters left by his giant feet.

◄ Elephants cool down by flapping their huge ears, which are lined with blood vessels.

▲ An elephant drinks about 60 gallons of water a day, enough to fill 240 milk cartons.

More elephants are walking toward the water hole. This is a herd of females. Mothers, daughters, and babies stay together as a family. Bull elephants usually live alone, until the females call to them using "infrasound," a low noise that humans cannot hear. Mother elephants with calves can be very dangerous, so we retreat to a safe distance. The smell of water is so exciting that the leading elephants break into a lumbering run. A baby follows, tripping over its own trunk. One by one, they arrive at the water's edge, lining up to drink like soldiers on parade.

▲ These thirsty zebras have traveled many miles to find water.

The Way to Dusty Death

Drinking is a risky business. A hungry lion may be lurking nearby. Crocodiles hide underwater, waiting to ambush a careless zebra or antelope. An elephant herd has nothing to fear, but most water hole visitors are nervous. They drink quickly, looking around carefully after every gulp.

By the end of the dry season, most water holes have shrunk to muddy puddles, crowded with thirsty and cranky animals. If the rains are late, they dry out completely. Everything living in the water is trapped. Hippos, too weak to walk far, slowly die. Amazingly, some fish survive. The lungfish can breathe air, even though it has gills like other fish. As the pool shrinks, it burrows down and makes a kind of mud cocoon, which is soon baked hard by the sun. Breathing through an air hole, it can live without water for months until the rains arrive.

▼ Months of drought can turn a large water hole like this into nothing but dried mud.

▼ Have you heard the gnus? The pounding hooves of galloping wildebeest kick up the dust.

A long period without rain turns the grassy plains into deserts. As food and water begins to dry out, some animals move to new feeding grounds. The annual wildebeest migration is one of the world's most famous journeys. Every year, a million wildebeest travel hundreds of miles across Africa. Thousands die along the way—killed by lions, eaten by crocodiles, drowned, or trampled underfoot. Others find their favorite route blocked by cattle fences, and simply starve to death.

▶ Bush fires cause panic in the animal kingdom, but new grass soon sprouts on the burned ground.

A drought causes other problems, too. As we walk back to camp, the setting sun is blotted out by smoke. It only takes one spark to start a fire when the land is bone-dry. A raging brush fire destroys everything in its path, including animals, trees, even villages. If the wind changes direction, our campsite will be in danger.

Wildlife in
Danger

Back in camp, we watch the distant brush fire while we eat supper, wondering how many animals have already died. Life in Africa is an endless struggle for survival. As well as finding food and avoiding predators, animals are faced with other problems like disease, drought, fire, and floods. But the most serious threat comes from humans.

For centuries, Africans killed animals only for food, taking no more than they needed. When other people settled in Africa, they started shooting wildlife for fun and called it sport. Millions of animals were massacred. Today most hunting is strictly controlled, but we are still killing too many animals.

Ivory hunters and poachers slaughter thousands of elephants and rhinos. Their tusks and horns are turned into fancy carvings, dagger handles, and potions, and sold for high prices. Leopards are still shot and skinned to make rugs or coats. Other animals are trapped and sold as pets, or end up in meat markets.

► Most of the beautiful markings on a leopard skin are like rosettes, not solid spots.

◄ A fully grown rhinoceros is built like an armored tank—but it has no protection against bullets.

In only three decades, Africa's black rhinoceros population has fallen from 70,000 to just 3,000 animals. Its cousin, the white rhinoceros, was rescued in the nick of time, just before it became extinct. Even with strict laws to protect them, saving the rhinos is very difficult. Someone suggested cutting off their horns so that the poachers would leave them alone. The plan failed. Whenever the poachers found that they had been following the tracks of a dehorned rhino, they killed it anyway, to avoid making the same mistake twice. No wonder we haven't seen a single rhinoceros during this journey.

The brush fire has burnt itself out, so it is safe to go to sleep. We crawl into our tents for the last time, remembering to check our sleeping bags for puff adders.

◄ The leopard tortoise is common, but other kinds of tortoise are almost extinct because of the pet trade.

▲ The tusks of this magnificent bull elephant make him a prime target for poachers.

Out of
Africa

This is our last morning in Africa. While breakfast is cooking, we pack up the tents. The dusty backpacks have to be beaten against a tree trunk. Something falls out and scurries under a rock. It looks like a small crab, but it has a tail with a hooked tip. How long has that scorpion been in the bag?

We hear thunder in the distance. Somewhere far away, a storm is brewing. This could be the start of the rainy season. The wildebeest migration has begun. It is time for us to leave, too. While we load the truck, Cisco buries the hot ashes from last night's fire. We don't want to start another brush fire. Finally, we make sure that we aren't leaving behind any litter.

◄ The golden rules on safari are to take nothing but photographs, and leave nothing but footprints.

◀ A bird's-eye view of our last African elephant.

Just a few hours later, we are in the air. Below us, an elephant walks through the swamp. From this distance, it seems to be moving in slow motion. Maybe it's the same one that we saw when we first arrived.

The plane passes over village after village. Fossils and bones found in Africa tell us that the first humans lived here thousands of years ago, before they spread to other parts of the world. Africa is a big place, but it has more people than ever before, and they all need space for their homes, farms, cattle, and crops. Elephants, antelopes, big cats, and the rest of the continent's wildlife need space too. In their own way, they are just as important. As Africa becomes more crowded, let's hope that we can find ways for wild animals and people to share the land and live side by side.

▲ The annual rains turn Africa's dry plains into lush grassland.

Glossary

Acacia Thorny tree with feathery leaves eaten by a variety of animals

Algae Miniature plants found in water

Baboon Large monkey with long, sharp teeth

Baobab Type of huge tree with a fat, water-filled trunk

Bat-eared fox Type of fox that hunts at night by using its large ears to listen for food

Bilharzia Tiny worm, found in water snails and dangerous to humans

Bush Area of wild, open spaces far away from towns and villages

Camouflage Disguise that helps an animal to hide

Carcass Dead animal

Cicada Noisy insect that calls loudly to find a mate

Clan Large group of hyenas

Drought Long period without rain

Egret Type of heron, usually with white feathers

Gnu Another name for a wildebeest

Gregarious Living in large flocks or herds

Grooming Keeping fur clean by removing dirt and parasites

Hamerkop Bird with a hammer-shaped head, famous for its enormous nest

Hide Skin of an animal

Honeyguide Type of bird famous for guiding people to bees' nests

Host Plant or animal on which a parasite feeds or lives

Impala Common kind of antelope found throughout Africa

Ivory Hard, white material such as elephant tusks

Jacana Water bird with enormous feet

Klipspringer Small antelope that lives on steep cliffs

Malaria Disease carried by some mosquitoes, causing fever or even death

Mamba Large, deadly, fast-moving African snake

Marabou Large stork that mainly eats dead meat

Matriarch Female leader of a large family of animals

Migration Long journey from one home to another

Monitor Type of very large lizard

Nomadic Moving from one area to another, rather than always living in the same place

Oxpecker Type of bird that eats the parasites found on cattle and wild animals

Parasite Plant or animal that feeds on another living plant or animal

Poacher Illegal hunter who kills animals, often for money

Predator Animal that hunts and kills other animals

Prey Animal that is killed and eaten by a predator

Pride Family of lions

Puff adder Poisonous snake that puffs out its body when disturbed

Python Large non-poisonous snake that kills by crushing its prey

Roller Brightly colored, acrobatic bird

Safari Swahili word for "journey"

Salt pan Large area of salt left behind after water evaporates

San Nomadic hunter-gatherers from Southern Africa

Sausage Tree Tree with red, bell-shaped flowers and huge sausage-shaped fruit

Scavenger Animal that eats scraps and rotten food such as dead meat

Shoebill Large, uncommon stork with a massive bill, also known as the whale-head

Swahili Language spoken in parts of East Africa

Talon Hooked claw

Termite Tiny insect that eats dead plants

Tick Blood-sucking mite that feeds on warm-blooded animals

Troop Large family of monkeys

Tsessebe Large, fast-running antelope

Tymbal Part of a cicada's body, used to produce a loud noise

Water hole Pool of water where animals gather to drink

Weaver Type of bird that builds a nest woven from grass or twigs

Wildebeest Large, ox-like African antelope

Index

Acknowledgments

All photos Tim Knight, except: Richard Clemence, pages 4/5 (children); Estée Knight, page 10, page 14 (circle), page 41 (circle); Anthony Bannister, © Gallo Images/CORBIS p35br; John Gosler Map artwork page 6. Additional thanks to: Aaron Chan; Sophie Conlon; Jessica Creak; Oriel Southwood; Harry Steyn; YHA Adventure Shops, Oxford